"100 Days, 100 Grand: Part 0 - Introduction and Day 0"

fourth UK edition 2020

First published in Great Britain in 2018 by Redpump Ltd

Copyright © Chris Worth 2018

The right of Chris Worth to be identified as the author of this work has been asserted in accordance with the Copyright, Designs and Patents Act 1988.

This original work contains images created for this work alone and no license is granted for reproduction. All images not original creations are either out of copyright or have been licensed for use from the respective rights holders.

This perfect bound print paperback partwork edition 4 of **100 Days, 100 Grand: Part 0 - Introduction and Day 0**:

ISBN 978-1-912795-08-6

The print edition of this book is set in 8 and 10pt Harriet and 10-26pt Frutiger. All typefaces licensed or purchased from **Linotype** and **Okay Type**.

All rights reserved. No part of this publication may be reproduced, transmitted, or stored in a retrieval system in any format other than its published form as authorised by the creator or by any other means without explicit permission in writing from Redpump Ltd or the author.

See amazon.com/author/chrisworth for works by this author, chrisdoescontent.com for the author's credentials and experience, or 100days100grand.com for book updates and reader offers.

"THE PURPOSE OF BUSINESS IS TO CREATE AND KEEP A CUSTOMER."

- Peter Drucker

100 DAYS, 100 GRAND EDITIONS

This is the partwork edition of **100 Days, 100 Grand**: the same content as the complete work, but split into 12 smaller books for ease of use. Collect the set (Kindle or paperback) or buy the complete work as one book. The Parts are:

- *Part 0: Introduction and Day 0*
- *Part 1: Choose your tools*
- *Part 2: Define your offer*
- *Part 3: Find your market*
- *Part 4: Build your network*
- *Part 5: The List*
- *Part 6: The Letter*
- *Part 7: The Campaign*
- *Part 8: Prospect to project*
- *Part 9: Project to customer*
- *Part 10: Customer to retainer*
- *Appendices and bonus material*

The complete book (UK edition) is in paperback as **100 Days, 100 Grand**, ISBN **978-0-9927470-4-6** and on Kindle as ISBN **978-0-9927470-3-9**.

See amazon.com/author/chrisworth for works by this author, chrisdoescontent.com for the author's credentials and experience, or 100days100grand.com for book updates and reader offers.

Figure 1: Don't feel trapped by life. Let's go six-figure freelancing.

100 DAYS, 100 GRAND: IS IT FOR YOU?

100 Days, 100 Grand is a step-by-step guide to earning £100,000+ from the skills you have now... *whatever they are*.

- *Define your **signature move** worth £100,000+ a year*
- *Create TWO £350,000 **business assets** in just 100 days*
- *Find 1,000 ideal **sales prospects**—without cold calls*
- *Win customers **10-20x faster** than professional marketers*
- *Gain 3-8 **repeat customers** paying you £8,350+/month*
- *Turn 1 in 2 projects into **monthly retainers** of £500-2,750+*
- *Charge rates **3-6x higher** than others doing the same job*

Turn your expertise into a six-figure freelance income...

Over 30m enterprising people earn six figures from what they do—in £, €, or $. They're not all bankers, doctors, and lawyers. Nor are they luckier, smarter, or harder working than you. They just focus on *finding the right market for what they do*... and take the results to the bank.

...in just 100 days—with easy-to-follow actions and tasks

Professionally designed and beautifully illustrated, **100 Days, 100 Grand** is a full-colour workbook by jetsetting London freelancer **Chris Worth**. Sharing methods honed on 1,000+ projects, its 100 short chapters—with *precise instructions and task lists for each day*—cover *everything* you need to earn a top-tier income from whatever you do best... and stay in that top 1% in the decades ahead.

100 Days, 100 Grand puts you in the top 1% of earners

No web scams, no penny stocks, no cold calling. Just easy-to-apply methods and actions in sequence: everything that works and nothing that doesn't. With no business infrastructure needed beyond a laptop and web connection.

Whether you change lives or lightbulbs for a living, if you want a six-figure income from it 100 days from now—this book is for you. For more information and resources, head for 100days100grand.com.

ACKNOWLEDGEMENTS

 Lots of people contributed to the scribbled sheaf of ideas that became **100 Days, 100 Grand**—many without knowing they did so. Special thanks to:

My wife **Lynne** and the **Chang** clan, for stories that span cultures; my parents **Brian** and **Carole** and sister **Stacey**, for always being there when I was far away; **Melissa** and **Maina** across the Atlantic, creative muses both Homeric and Platonic; singing accountant and longtime friend **Neil Goulder**, a worked example of "Don't worry, be happy"; global citizen **Tom O'B Baker**, for wise words since Tokyo; artist **Michelle Abrahall**, for colouring inside the lines; and **Joel Uden** for the best proofreading of all—actually doing the book.

In business and academia: the past masters of **advertising** like Hopkins, Ogilvy, Sullivan, and Kennedy, and their books that taught me how to earn like a pro on the life of a poet; consultant **Michael Porter** for making business make sense; **Dan Kahnemann** for working out what makes people tick; **Mihaly Csikszentmihalyi** and **Cal Newport** for flow and deep work; **Brian Greene** for describing how breathtaking reality might be; **Ray Dalio** for summarising his life's learnings in two books; **Andrew Matthews** for Being Happy. It just works.

In art and lit: **James Joyce**, for showing how far English could go; **Ernest Hemingway**, who did the same from the opposite end; **Hunter S Thompson**, who blitzed both in a blender; the **Italian Futurist** and **Bauhaus Modernist** schools, for honing a country boy's sense of beauty; the creators and characters of **100 Bullets** and **Watchmen** for writing a world more real.

In fitness and in health: **Paul "Coach" Wade**, **Pavel "Kettlebell" Tsatsouline**, and brothers **Danny** and **Al Kavadlo** for the training programmes that deliver lifelong awesomeness; **Fitsz Dubova** and the cast and crew of the **Commando Temple**, the galaxy's coolest workout space. All you need is a bar and a bell.

Elsewhere: business consultant action hero **Gabe Rayner**, for showing me where extreme self-actualisation can lead; my alma mater **Warwick Business School** (wbs.ac.uk) for letting someone who dropped out of school at 16 give its world-ranked MBA a go; my **clients** down the decades, for trusting briefs and budget to a guy in jeans and T.

Finally, to moral philosopher **Ayn Rand** (aynrand.org) for defining the only system of values that makes sense.

DISCLAIMER

100 Days, 100 Grand is based on the author's experiences, and is provided on an as-is basis without representations as to its effectiveness for you. If you buy and/or read this creative work, you agree to hold the author and his associates and businesses harmless in regard to any and all reputational, monetary, consequential, and other losses suffered by you at all times in any way whatsoever, and to comply with and be bound by these terms and conditions.

- *The contents of this book are for your personal use only and subject to change without notice. You may not reproduce, reformat, republish, or offer instruction in its methods by any means unless expressly authorised by the author.*
- *Neither the author, his associates and businesses, nor any third party provides any warranty or guarantee as to the accuracy, timeliness, performance, completeness or suitability of the information found in this book or its related properties.*
- *You acknowledge that such information and materials may contain inaccuracies or errors and that liability for any such is excluded to the fullest extent permitted by law. Your use of any information or materials in this book or its associated resources is entirely at your own risk and it is your own responsibility to ensure any actions, events or outcomes are legal.*
- *This book contains copyrighted material including, but not limited to, design, layout, get-up, illustrations, and instructions. Reproduction is prohibited other than in accordance with the copyright notice, which forms part of these conditions. All trademarks reproduced in this book are the property of their respective owners and no licensing to or ownership by the reader is given or implied.*
- *This book includes links to information and materials not created by the author. No guarantee, warranty, or endorsement of these is given or implied. Your use of this book is subject to UK law and any dispute arising shall be subject to UK courts in accordance with UK legislation.*

This book is an original work and all rights including copyright in all media are asserted and reserved by the creator. All images not original creations have been released or licensed by their rights holders or are out of copyright. All methods not developed by the author are credited to their creators.

CONTENTS

"The purpose of business is to create and keep a customer." 3
100 DAYS, 100 GRAND EDITIONS 5
100 DAYS, 100 GRAND: IS IT FOR YOU? 7
ACKNOWLEDGEMENTS 8
DISCLAIMER 9
ERRATA 11
FOREWORD: PIRSIG'S BRICK 12
WHAT THIS BOOK'S ABOUT 14
...AND WHAT IT ISN'T 15
INTRO: CUSTOMERS WITHOUT LIMIT 16
STAYING MOTIVATED 21
WHAT YOU NEED 25
HOW THIS BOOK WORKS 26
..."What I do isn't worth that!" 33
   Day 0: Plan out the plan 35
ABOUT THE AUTHOR 43
INDEX 44
LIST OF FIGURES 46

ERRATA

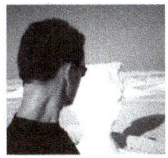Before you start: **this book contains errors**. It was edited with a critical eye and proofread practically with a loupe, but ultimately it's the work of one guy with a laptop. Meaning most of the actual content emerged from gaps on the calendar, a Himalayan stack of scribbled notes, and frantic bouts of self-doubt on the pullup bar. (Not to mention the 1,000 empty bottles in the green bin.)

Happy wine merchants aside, any first edition of a textbook spanning three years of work will retain some scars and scuffs from 70+ rounds of writing and revising. Doubly so when there's 1,200 pages and 300,000 words of it. Mostly minor, and there are (probably) no fails epic enough to fry the methodology, but to err is human. All errors are the fault of the author, alone, so for any and all typographical tangles: apologies.

Here's the positive for readers on Kindle: whenever an error is reported at 100days100grand.com/errata, **the Kindle editions will be first to benefit**. So if you spot a mistake—even if it's just a typo—please submit it. Thanks!

Kindle readers can get updates free from *manage your content and devices* at their Amazon account. (Make sure Whispersync is turned on so you don't lose your Notes and Highlights.) And, of course, check out the extra information and resources at 100days100grand.com.

FOREWORD: PIRSIG'S BRICK

In Zen and the Art of Motorcycle Maintenance, one of narrator Robert Pirsig's students is in trouble. She's been asked to write 500 words on the USA and her mind's a blank. Problem? The subject's too big, too broad. She can't find that hook that gets her started.

So Phaedrus tells her to go to a building on Main Street and try again . . . *starting with the upper-left-hand brick*. The next day she's back—with five thousand words on paper.

Pirsig's Brick is why I wrote this book.

In decades working for myself, I've met thousands of people like that student, across hundreds of professions. People with the skills to earn an income in the top 1%, if they just *knew where to start*.

They're not just people you commonly think of as freelancers, like contractors, copywriters, and consultants. All *sorts* of job descriptions have indies in their orbit, including those you probably think are salaried roles. Soccer players. Delivery drivers. Financial advisors. Art experts. Wine dealers. Paralegals. Teachers. Caregivers. Martial arts instructors. Surf school bums. People who guide others through insurance mazes. Act as patient advocates. Tutor others in lost languages. Write ultra-niche software. Set up buying clubs. Make artisan cheese. Repurpose found objects. These are people with ambition and creativity and expertise, developed over decades.

Trouble is, most don't earn an income that matches those skills. (Some don't even hit *minimum wage*.) It's not for want of trying. They'd all *like* to be among those freelancers who always seem abuzz with projects, own a humming sales pipeline, a bursting order book. Remember this: those people only have it together because they had a **Pirsig's Brick**. Something that *got them started*.

And with the step-by-step plan in **100 Days, 100 Grand**, you can join them.

Think of **Day 1** as your upper-left-hand brick. That chapter and the 99 that follow get rid of the stumbling blocks, with a concise set of tasks to complete between dawn and dusk over 100 days. Each day taking you 24 hours closer to a singular goal: *earning a six-figure income from the skills you have now*. Even if you've never freelanced before.

That's what prompted this book. Like all freelancers, I've had good years and bad years. 100 Days, 100 Grand is the result of noting down what led to the *good* years . . . and the differences that made them *great*. It started as my own work plan to improve my freelancing; it was only some way in I realised other people might find it useful too.

The methods and models ahead draw on the experiences of over 100 clients and 1,000 projects in a portfolio that spans 20+ years working in 16 markets across Europe, Asia, and North America. It includes everything that led to success in finding and keeping real customers . . . and nothing that didn't. In other words, I made the mistakes so you don't have to.

Of course, it isn't just freelancers who buy this book—I've even heard of salaried salespeople using these methods to build their book of customers and plan their quarterly activities. But since *I'm* a freelancer, it's aimed more at the indie set than anyone else. Because I believe it's the freelance professional who'll get the most bang per buck from **100 Days, 100 Grand**.

As a freelance copywriter, I use all these methods myself, in the same sequence. And expect to continue doing so. (There's not a lot of money in writing workbooks.) So while on one level it's a general set of principles and practices, on another level it's deeply personal. Time will tell if I've got the balance right.

This book's for you if you want to work your own hours, on your own terms, doing work you enjoy, for people who appreciate it. Living a life true to yourself, with a high income, low costs, and a positive sense of purpose.

Let's face it, life's too short to live any other way.

Figure 2: The author and a few friends, somewhere above California

CHRIS WORTH

Visit **100 Days, 100 Grand** at http://100days100grand.com

WHAT THIS BOOK'S ABOUT...

This book is a step-by-step guide to earning an annual income of £100,000+ with the professional skills you have now . . . *whatever they are*.

It's not a dreamy wishlist of abstract ideas, but *practical* and *concrete* instructions telling you **what to do**, **each day**, for **one hundred days**. With daily time estimates and checklists to keep you on track. Life doesn't come with an instruction book—but earning a top-tier income now does. Drawing on the author's experiences acquiring and retaining over 1,000 freelance projects with over 100 clients across 16 countries and markets, **100 Days, 100 Grand** is everything that works, and nothing that doesn't.

The text is organised as 100 short chapters. Each contains around 1,000 words of content and another 1,000 of tasks. At the end—if you've done it all—your income will equal an annualised £100,000. In other words, you'll be bringing in fees of £8,350 a month plus.

You might think you can do it faster. If so, great. There's a rhythm to the way this stuff works, moving through topics in 1-3 hour chunks, and each chapter is timed to take one day of reasoned effort for most people. Feel free to try it in 50 if you like early mornings and late nights.

(Or you might do it slower. If you leave a week between days, be prepared to work harder to get back on track. Contractors call it the "pick-up / put-down" problem; you'll learn how to solve it forever on **Day 93**.)

It's also about getting to that £100,000 figure at **low cost**. After all, the office of many freelancers is their kitchen table and their biz dev budget wouldn't even fold. So this book doesn't ask any more business infrastructure than a laptop, web connection, and some everyday software. Your investment comes from your head and hands, not your bank account.

And finally, it's about **smart use of technology**. There's no coding or financial whizzbangery ahead, but it does assume a working knowledge of computers and common office software. If you can use a web browser, word processor, and spreadsheet, and know some of the bigger web names like **LinkedIn** and **Google**, you're already there.

...AND WHAT IT ISN'T

This book *isn't* about the "hardware" of freelancing: registering a company, hiring an accountant, completing your tax return. These are the mechanics of running a small business, and they matter a lot. But *they're not the parts that get you earning*. (And there are countless resources out there for dealing with that stuff, anyway.)

Nor is it a "get rich quick" scheme. In fact, it laughs in the face of the money-for-nothing crowd. The 100-day plan doesn't involve trading currencies, dodgy property purchases, or selling to your friends. Leave those to the scammers and those fool enough to follow them.

The actions you'll take over 100 days to find and keep customers aren't new. They're tried-and-tested tactics *known to work*. Methods and models developed down the decades across businesses of all kinds . . . and used today to build sales in the billions. **100 Days, 100 Grand** uses what works. (Except cold calling. Cold calling *sucks*.)

It's not a dip-in reference book. The Days, and the Tasks within them, are designed to be approached *in order*. Reaching a £100,000 income is a work project like any other—and executing it involves a sequence of deliberate inputs and outcomes over time. This isn't a random grab-bag of tips.

It's not about residual income, either. (Income you earn in your sleep, like the payments actors, writers, and musicians get when you buy their work.) This isn't trash-talking residuals: royalties and commissions are *great*, and you may find opportunities for earning them once your freelance business gets rolling. But this book concentrates on **fee income**: doing a job where you'll be paid once for your time, with a project fee or day rate. Simply because that's how most freelancers work.

And lastly, it's not a "self-help" book. The power of positive thinking or being a highly effective person are both good ambitions, but if you've bought this book you probably have an upbeat attitude towards your life and work anyway.

And that's all you need. Because—as you're about to find out—the global economy can provide everything else.

INTRO: CUSTOMERS WITHOUT LIMIT

Once upon a time, wealth meant commodities. Wood, grains, skins, salt: stuff you found in the forest or peeled off a beast. Then value shifted from resources to processes: carpentry, baking, weaving, preserving. The first phase lasted millions of years. The second, a few thousand.

In the last few decades, there's been *another* great shift. And it's the most thrilling yet. A move away from commodities, away even from adding value by processing them. It's a shift that replaces *stuff* with *smarts*.

BUSINESS IS SUPERABUNDANCE . . .

Cars today go further and faster, yet use less steel. Buildings reach for the skies, yet use less concrete. Planes carry more people, yet burn less fuel. And some of the most competitive products and services out there—in technology, software, and communications—add value with dots: electrons and photons.

Innovation and expertise are supplanting raw resources. And unlike stuff you dig out of the ground, **human creativity** is in infinite supply.

This is the global economy today. Where wealth is created by *human potential*, applying your ideas and skills in a connected market for a share of the value you create. It's not scarcity. Not even abundance. But **superabundance**.

. . . AND CUSTOMERS ARE EVERYWHERE

Open borders, free markets, and connected economies make this world of superabundance rich with options for one category of worker: the **freelance professional**. And the sheer *breadth* of opportunities is stunning.

North America and Europe each contain 350 million of the world's wealthiest consumers. Other nations with huge populations—a hundred million each in Vietnam and the Philippines, even more in Mexico, Brazil, and Indonesia, a billion-plus in both India and China—contain vast and unmined cultural and intellectual riches. And the people of Australia, Canada, and Russia dwell atop unimaginable natural resources and billions of acres of land.

The *smallest* company in the Fortune 500 turns over US$5bn a year; the financial markets of the USA, UK, and EU list companies valued in the *trillions*. In the UK, over 15,000 companies have turnovers above £100m and a payroll of over 250 people; Germany's *Mittelstand* is home to over 1,300 SMEs, each in its sector's top three. 6m US companies employ over 100m Americans; another 60m are freelancers. More than 20 countries have a GDP of over a trillion US dollars, all buzzing in a connected global economy of over a *hundred* trillion.

In Africa, a billion people are opening borders and businesses in spite of governments; across the Pacific, another 600m trade across the archipelago of Southeast Asia. The tigers of Hong Kong, Singapore, Taiwan, and South Korea feast on the giant markets of China, Japan, Europe, and America, adding value everywhere. While China—its credit financing the world—is the economic story of the century... and perhaps the only one that matters.

So why, given this rainforest of opportunities, do so many freelancers have trouble extracting just £100,000—the aim of **100 Days, 100 Grand**—from it?

The problem isn't a shortage of stuff to do, or a paucity of businesses to connect with. It's not even the number of competitors. It's navigating the confusion of opportunities out there... to find the right customers for *you*.

YOUR SKILLS ARE SALEABLE...

If you're lucky enough to live in the rich nations of the West or the tigers of the East, you're already a winner in the opportunity lottery. But there are so *many* companies out there already, and so *many* relationships between them, it's common for freelancing newbies to wonder if there are any customers left over. Are there? **Yes**. Because **superabundance isn't a zero-sum game**.

This rich and dense network doesn't just *contain* new opportunities; it *creates* them. In a superabundant economy, *whatever* your area of expertise—from sweeping streets to transforming industries—there are 3-8 customers out there (the numbers **100 Days, 100 Grand** uses) willing to pay for it.

Find a way to save people money, drive their sales, boost their profit margins, solve their business pain, or just give them an easier life, and you've got a market to exploit.

... IF YOU CONNECT TO THE RIGHT COMPANIES

If the number of businesses out there and the density of connections between them keep increasing, it means *more* customers for you, not fewer. (Even if the number of competitors keeps growing too.) And you don't need many repeat clients to earn a top-1% income. It's all about **making the right connections**.

Not making the right connections is the reason so many freelancers live on crumbs thrown by a former employer. Why so many try it for a couple of years, then crawl back to a cube farm and daily commute. But it's also why *other* freelancers—let's say the top 1%—seem to find great clients and make six figures almost effortlessly. The difference: the former *let* things happen, the latter *make* things happen.

100 Days, 100 Grand is the make-things-happen part.

30 MILLION PEOPLE ARE DOING IT ALREADY

Around the world, tens of millions of people enjoy an upper-income lifestyle without ever needing to employ people, make risky investments, or maintain costly infrastructure. They do it with a minimalist approach: keeping things simple and concentrating on the basics.

This book is big on simple. It's a sequence of deliberate actions for tracking down the companies and people of most value to you, connecting with them, and turning them into customers one by one. No cold calling, no Ponzi schemes, no buying lists... but no shortcuts, either.

By completing its tasks and hitting its targets, you will—not might, *will*—end up earning £8,350+ each month in freelance fees. An income near the top 1% of salaries in any developed economy, even the richest ones.

SO WHAT'S THE CATCH?

Bluntly: you have to work at it. This isn't a self-help manual; it's a work plan. (Although there's a fair dose of fun, too.) So before you start, look inside yourself and ask: *do you really want this?*

Because becoming a top-1% freelancer isn't a free lunch. The next 100 days mean hitting your desk (or kitchen table) each morning and not powering down until dusk. If you want it, work for it. But if you do, the rewards are huge.

Approached the right way, professional freelancing gives you a broader outlook and greater freedom than most people will ever experience. The ability to take a year off to work on your novel. Go back to school for that Master's degree. Or drop out for months at a time, hitting the road with a backpack and credit card. Knowing you can build a six-figure income in 100 days gives you the confidence to do whatever you want. That's what this book delivers.

WHY 100 GRAND, ANYWAY?

First, it's within the potential of—well, anyone. Over thirty million people make an income in six figures, whether it's dollars, pounds or euros. You won't be lounging on a superyacht or Learing weekly to Manhattan—but who needs yachts and planes? They're the fastest-depreciating assets around. (If you want the feeling of owning a boat, stand over a storm drain tearing up banknotes.) And while 100 days isn't jam by Friday, it's only a quarter of a year or so. You can plan for completion because the end date's already in sight, without losing energy because the horizon seems too far away.

Whether you're a tech-savvy professional with an MBA, or a dreaming chancer who dropped out in his teens—the author is both—there *are* customers who'll pay top dollar for what you do, if you present your offer in the right way.

By applying the right actions in logical sequence, *anyone* with professional skills can earn a six-figure annual income. And get there on a set schedule: *100 days from now*.

DO IT BECAUSE YOU CAN

Take a moment to think about that world of superabundance again.

For pennies a day, those in developed nations (and many developing ones) have instant access to every bright idea ever written down, every expert with a laptop, every answer ever needed. All the Great Works of science, philosophy, and literature now fit in your pocket. Some of the greatest universities put their course materials online for *free*.

Our planet now has more mobile connections than people. Billions use the web, swap emails, share documents, instant message, video chat, play games, share experiences. Social media are bringing people and cultures together; relational databases, cloud computing, and machine learning are making sense of Big Data. Streaming and subscribing have replaced broadcasting and channelsurfing; thin tablets have outevolved bulky books; crowdfunding and cryptocurrencies are redefining finance. Supercomputers in your pocket and ecosystems of apps are making life footloose and frictionless for millions. And the software applications, business processes, programming languages, and searchable resources the web enables make building a business easy, scaling your services simple, and communicating with customers cheap.

With most of the world's population now connected by wires and waves, your market may span *hundreds of millions of people*. And you only need to bite off the tiniest fraction of it to prosper. This superabundant economy offers you an *infinite* range of things to do, stuff to learn, and customers to engage with—*if* you use the right methods, with the right attitude.

The world is yours. *If* you want it. **And on that note** . . .

Figure 3: Bocconi's "Unique Forms". A solid market offer.

STAYING MOTIVATED

The next 100 days will be hard work. When you wake up, you'll find many reasons to miss a day, or skip a chapter because you learnt this stuff in b-school. *Especially* when the core Parts **1-4** are done, and you clock on for the critical thinking of **Part 5** and the bubbling creativity of **Part 6**.

You'll need to push on. This isn't a self-help manual. It's a **work plan**: practical methods known to succeed. The decision to commit and complete must come from you. Here are a few tips that'll help you stick at it.

MAKE A CONTRACT WITH YOUR FUTURE SELF

A vague plan to "get fit" will lead to joining a gym, going twice, then giving up. But entering a distant desert race and booking non-refundable tickets is a commitment to reach a certain level of fitness by a certain date. You've made a contract with your future self.

These agreements are called **Ulysses contracts**—after the ancient Greek who lashed himself to a mast before passing the Sirens, knowing his future self wouldn't be able to resist the urge to sail onto the rocks. And you can motivate yourself for your 100 Days quest the same way. Set yourself a goal you can't back out of, something that'll *hurt* if you don't succeed.

It's human nature to give up when things get hard or dull. (And they will.) It's one reason **100 Days, 100 Grand** hews to a 100-day structure with concrete actions and tasks. If you commit to not going out or getting distracted until each chapter's done each day, that's your 9AM self making a contract with your 7PM self. A series of small contracts can work just as well as one big £100,000 contract. Decide which works best for you, but *make that commitment*.

START EACH DAY WITH A RITUAL

To maintain motivation day after day, do something—anything—to set yourself up first thing in the morning. In the second half of the 100 days ahead, many days consist of repeating tasks and adding context to actions already completed; it's hard work. But *that's the way success happens*.

Some people meditate. Others work out. Some need a short shock, like an icy shower. (No thanks.) It doesn't matter what it is, but try to do *something* to get yourself in the mood each morning. (See **Plan your CPD** at the end for some more ideas on keeping your skills sharp.)

MAKE LISTS FOR EVERYTHING

It's amazing how much control you can gain over your life by writing things down. So another useful habit to develop is **making lists**.

With a list, it's easier to see where you're expending energy needlessly. (Days **95** and **96** give the why.) And there's no satisfaction like checking-completed-items-off-a-list satisfaction. So make lists *all the time*. Whatever you need to do, buy, or create, make a list, in logical sequence from start to finish.

It's how this book's organised: an action plan and a checklist, every day. Getting in the habit of making lists helps in life, not just at work.

DIVIDE YOUR TIME INTO CHUNKS

Little carrots and sticks help you complete your daily task list. Try structuring the day into units of an hour or two, then write those blocks of time into your calendar and *don't let yourself off the hook*. (See **Day 0** in this book for an approach you can use.)

Doing this combines a stick with a carrot: you can set reasonable hours to work each day—perhaps 10-1 in the morning and 2-5 in the afternoon. (Six hours a day is an average estimate for the time 100 days will take.) No 18-hour stints, no pulling all-nighters. Just manageable stretches of focussed **deep work**. (Deep work's a theme of **Part 2**.)

Learning to treat your calendar as your master—building time awareness and deadline discipline—carries immense benefit to freelancers, who don't have their days structured by someone else. Organise your time effectively, and you can fit a *lot* of work into a day.

> **SIDEBAR: Small goals, small scale**
>
> Many self-help books tell you to "set big goals". But while dreamy wanderings of the imagination may be fun, no big goal is achievable unless broken into a series of *small* actions.

So this book concentrates on the *little* goals. Tasks and outcomes that fit into a few hours a day, building up practices and habits over time, repeated until practice makes perfect. Little goals add up.

Big goals get you dreaming; small goals get you started

If you're unfit, you could say you'll run a marathon someday. Or you could jog around the block *now*. If you want to speak French, you could get disheartened with Flaubert . . . or you could start learning *three words a day*. If you're broke, a little goal of saving £10/month puts you on the right track to adjusting your whole attitude towards money.

Earning £8,350+ each month isn't so much a stretch goal as a *habit to develop*. Over the next 100 days you'll develop it, by executing all the tasks and reaching the daily outcomes on each day's checklist. That's what this book aims to drill into your daily routine: the habits of six-figure freelancing.

Scaling up is not a freelancer's goal

Open any big-bad business book, and you'll see a lot about **scale**. Growing your business; amortising costs; enabling higher profit margins. These are all good things. But 100 Days *isn't* about scale.

Because you know what scale is? It's the point where you can't deal with things as an *individual*. And dealing with things as an individual is the whole value proposition of freelancing.

As an individual freelancer, you don't want—or need—scale. You're not in the Fortune 500, and your customers don't want you to be. Your appeal to your market is contained in *who you are*. And the best way to communicate that is to *be yourself* in all your dealings with customers.

You don't *need* customer relationship management geekware to build a roster of 3-8 clients. (One of your goals for the next 100 days.) You don't *need* inbound marketing wizardry to put 1,000 names into your sales funnel. (Although some of its ideas will help.) And you don't *need* to plan out a twelve-touch customer journey to hit a 1% conversion rate. At the scale of the individual freelancer, you achieve these goals with proven methods, critical thinking . . . and the content and tasks in this book. Your tools are simple: laptop and broadband, Excel and Word, a website or two. (Or whatever equivalents you prefer.)

That's zero scale. But it's also zero distance between you and your customers. And zero distance lets you build business relationships that are deeper and more personal than any consumer has with a big-box brand name.

STOP AND THINK EACH DAY . . .

If you want that six-figure income—not just this year, but every year—you'll have to make the practices in this book your daily habits. (Beyond 100 days it's about maintaining and iterating, not building from scratch.)

Again, that's hard work, so make sure it doesn't take over your life. Set aside an hour each day for working on your *business* and another hour for working on *yourself*: the stuff that improves your health, wealth, and happiness. Climb walls. Do Yoga. Go for a swim. Read an author you've never tried. Do a calculation in your head. Explore a street you've never walked down. Above all, remember leisure is just as important as work. Finally . . .

. . . AND DO IT *IN* 100 DAYS!

This book is structured as a 100-day work plan, each chapter a day's work. Because dealing with a defined set of tasks in a single day lets you warm up and cool down properly—crossing off a checklist at sundown and then *stopping*, with a sense of completion. Without the pick-up / put-down problem of one day's Tasks spilling over into the next day.

Of course, that doesn't mean you have to block a straight 100 days on your calendar. You could schedule it over 200 days to fit around your job, working on 100 Days every *other* day. Or do it in a year of weekends. What matters is that you approach it *in sequence*.

Why? Because each chapter depends on the chapters before it. This book isn't a dip-in reference; it's a series of actions building towards a goal. Miss a day, or not finish a Task because you didn't see the point, and there'll be trouble ahead. So try to maintain steady discipline as you work through.

Thankfully, not all chapters will take every hour between sunrise and sunset. Take **Part 1**. The first week's all about basic tools and concepts. If you know them already, you might complete each chapter in a couple of hours! But it'll help if you take the rest of the day to let each concept sink in properly.

At the other end of the scale, in the more busywork-filled Parts (**5-7**) it'll be tempting to fall behind on your figures and daily totals, since some repeating Tasks take several hours each day. Discipline again. Once you've decided your schedule, **try not to let it slip**.

Whatever timescale you complete it on, plan on 100 Days *taking* 100 days, one after the other. No less—but no more.

WHAT YOU NEED

What does this book ask of you? It asks a certain amount of get-up-and-go. (But you've got that already, right?) It asks a bit of creative thinking—but everyone's creative, even if you think you're not. And it asks you to get to grips with a few basic b-school concepts in Parts **1-4**, plus some hard work with spreadsheets and documents.

The skills this book *doesn't* teach are the ones you probably used to find it. How to use a computer and web browser, the basics of web search and social networks, a couple of office applications. Here's a list.

You'll need some sort of **calendar** and **contact manager**. Microsoft Outlook, Apple Calendar, Google Calendar, and plain pencil and paper all work. (A **Google** account is part and parcel of the next 100 days; you'll set one up in **Part 1** if you don't have one already.)

You'll need a **word processor**. The go-to is Microsoft Word. But Google's **Docs** works in much the same way. While if you're into text editors like vi and emacs, you've got way more skills than you need for your 100-day plan.

You'll need a **spreadsheet**. This book uses Microsoft Excel, but Google **Sheets** again works fine, as does LibreOffice on Linux.

But the main thing you'll bring to your 100-day party is even cheaper: the **right frame of mind**. Because while the methods in this book don't use anywhere near the juice of today's web wrangling, word processing, and spreadsheet sorting applications, they do involve a *different way of thinking*. A deeper view of what these apps do . . . and how to make the most of them.

Finally, if you're *truly* starting from zero, **all the tools are available free**. Your local library or university may offer internet access; Linux and LibreOffice cost nothing to download; Google Docs and Sheets are free to play around with.

So if you're in a hard place financially, give silent thanks to the people who created the tools you're going to build a £100,000 income from in the next year . . . and use them to the full. And **don't forget to donate something back when you're earning**.

HOW THIS BOOK WORKS

Your 100-day plan is divided into ten **Parts**, each with a theme. Within each Part are **Days** (chapters). A **Part** is one or two weeks (7 or 14 **Days**) of mostly learning and doing Mon-Fri, and mostly reviewing and critiquing at weekends. (Yes, to complete in 100 days, you'll need to work weekends.)

The actions of each **Day** build on each other over time—basic actions at first, then connected sequences of decisions as you get deeper in. For instance, if you're learning about search spaces on Tuesday of **Part 1**'s week, you'll build on search on successive Tuesdays. Splitting these actions across time gives you breathing space to catch up and practice, letting the methods bed in properly over your 100 days.

INFORMATIONAL AND INSTRUCTIONAL CONTENT

Each chapter has two sections: **informational** and **instructional** content. Think of it as first reading, then doing.

Informational content

A day starts with **informational** content. It's a bit of textbook-style teaching, divided into numbered sections detailing the **methods** and **models** that'll get you from zero to £8,350+ in monthly billings.

People experienced in marketing and technology—those with their own websites, or who use Excel and Word every day—will use the informational content but skim the instructional, adapting the content to whatever methods or models they prefer. Think of informational content as a **broad strategy** you can customise.

Instructional content

While informational content is **strategic,** the **instructional** parts are **tactical**. Divided into numbered Tasks, they give you the sequence of actions to perform each day, down to the cells of your **List** and the paragraphs of your **Letter**. The tasks in each Day are a tried-and-tested work plan for *executing* what you learned from the informational content that precedes them.

Instructional content is for those expert in their own area, but less schooled in marketing and technology. The instructional parts are your How-To manual. Taken together with informational content, it means you'll never have to wonder "How do I do *that*?"

EACH DAY HAS THE SAME STRUCTURE

All chapters start with a **summary** of what you'll do and learn that day, and end with a **checklist**. The former to make sure you understand the **methods** taught, and the latter to keep you on track with the daily **Tasks**.

When you complete multi-part Tasks that span days or weeks, you'll see attaboys like **milestones** in the text. They're there to cheer you up and give you a sense of progress. (As are the clock graphics at the start of each **Part**, ticking their way to **Day 100**.)

MILESTONE REACHED!
Learned how **100 Days, 100 Grand** is structured.

Later on, you'll see that some Tasks repeat daily. This book deliberately breaks down big chunks of work, like list-building, into shorter sessions you complete bit by bit over many days. (Making 3 LinkedIn connections a day only takes half an hour—but think how that adds up over a few months.)

EACH PART'S INPUTS LEAD TO THE NEXT'S OUTPUTS

100 Days, 100 Grand is sequential: each chapter builds on the last. The basic methods you learn in **Part 1** are used to greater effect in Parts **2-4**, while the searching and scoring in **Part 5** come into their own in Parts **6-7**. And the sales funnel you learn on **Day 6** becomes your key tool for managing prospects in Parts **7-10** and beyond **Day 100**, when you're a true six-figure freelancer.

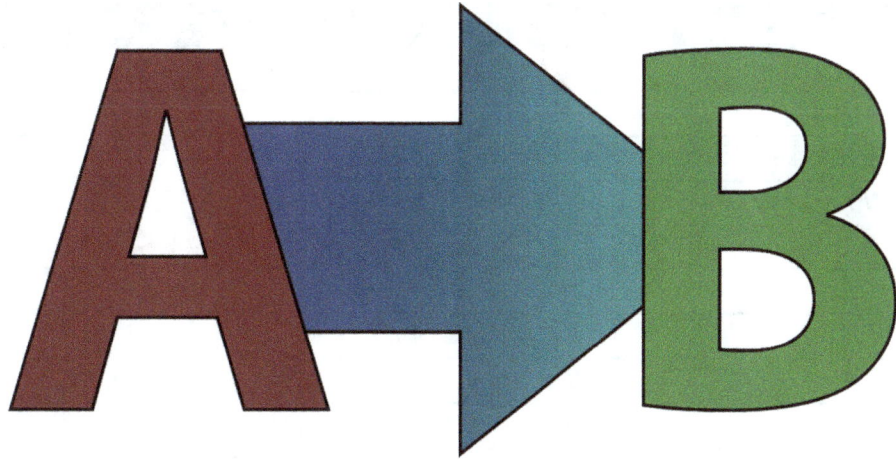

The same applies to finer-grained detail. The sales headline you write on **Day 1** becomes the basis of your positioning in **Part 2**. In **Part 5** the **selectors** you score are the plan for the **sales copy** you'll write in **Part 6**. And so on.

In each chapter's **Checklist**, there's a note of what you'll take forward from that Day, in **Takeouts**. While the **Totals** for each day give you a sense of how far you've come. Not guidelines, but actual numbers chosen to reflect typical ambitions for a freelance roster: 3-8 repeat clients, each paying you between £500 and £2,750 a month at and beyond **Day 100**.

All this is a friendly warning not to miss days or take shortcuts. Everything's connected. The less you miss, the better you'll do.

CHECKLISTS KEEP YOUR WORK ON TRACK

Checklists are a basic tool of any large project, whether it's building a skyscraper or flying a jumbo. They tell you whether you're doing the right things at the right time—and if not, what you need to do to correct it.

This book uses a three-part checklist for each day. The first part checks your understanding of the informational content in each Day, headlined **Do you understand**. The second part, **Have you completed**, deals with your Tasks and adds guideline timings for how long each should take. There's a note on what you take away from each chapter in **Takeouts**, then the last part keeps running **Totals** for your 100 days, tracking how many potential customers you've taken down the **sales funnel** you'll meet on **Day 6**.

(A sales funnel is how you'll build and manage your £8,350+ monthly revenue stream and keep it rolling beyond your hundred days. Ultimately, your 3-8 repeat clients by **Day 100** are just the outcome of building a **List** of 1,000 cold suspects starting **Day 0**.)

Here's what **Day 1**'s checklist looks like. It's quite short, since most of **Day 1** is about familiarising yourself with business networking:

CHECKLIST: DAY 1	
DO YOU UNDERSTAND:	
How to set up a LinkedIn profile	
How LinkedIn connects the 5 levels of the broader economy	
Why a headline needs to state what you do and for who	
HAVE YOU COMPLETED:	
1 hr	Set up your LinkedIn profile
1 hr	Chosen your profile photo
2 hrs	Written your sales headline
15 mins	Added 1 prospect to your **List**
TAKEOUTS:	
Sales headline.	
TOTALS:	
Companies found	1
People listed	0

However, take a look at **Day 96**, towards the end of your 100 days:

CHECKLIST: DAY 96	
DO YOU UNDERSTAND:	
The difference between **urgent and important**	
How a **six-hour workday** can work	
HAVE YOU COMPLETED:	
20 mins	Plotted your To-Do list on the Urgent versus Important diagram and rescheduled your work
30 mins	Made 2 connections on LinkedIn
30 mins	Added 2 prospects to your **List**
10 mins	Scored today's prospects for descriptor criteria
10 mins	Sent 3 Letters
15 mins	Followed up 1 hot prospect
15 mins	Sent out any acceptance notes, T's & C's, contact reports, success notes, and invoices
15 mins	Updated your sales funnel
1 hr	Reviewed and revised your **Letter**
4 hrs	Worked on your tenth project
1 hr	Written, costed, and split your fifth retainer agreement into contract and non-contract deliverables; issued retainer agreement to client
2 hrs	Worked on other client business
TAKEOUTS:	
5th retainer agreement. Work plan. Campaign047.	
TOTALS:	
Connections made	346
Companies found	300
People listed	996
Letters sent	996
FUNNEL:	
Cold suspects	0
Warm leads	899
Hot prospects	66
Qualified buyers	21
Confirmed customers	6
Repeat clients	3

As you progress in your 100 days, the checklists contain more and more items, breaking down the total Contacts you've made and Letters you've sent into the different stages of the sales funnel. To stay on track, check your work against the checklists. Every day.

THE ILLUSTRATED FREELANCER

The model uses some numbers common among successful freelancers: 3-8 repeat clients each paying a monthly retainer of £500-£2,750, with an £8,350 monthly income as your **Day 100** goal. It involves building a **List** of 1,000 prospects (**Part 5**) moving down your **sales funnel** in six **stages** (**Day 6**).

Your **List** and sales funnel may involve different numbers from the book's model, depending on what business you're in. So from **Part 5** you'll rely less on the model case, and more on what you put in your *own* spreadsheet. Just refer to the numbers that work for you; your daily *actions* will be the same. (There are countless routes to £100,000, from a single client paying £8,350 a month to a thousand-plus subscribers paying £8.)

As your 100 days march on, each day contains more repeated tasks and fewer new concepts, with each day's checklist giving you running totals and a crib sheet for checking your knowledge. Of course, in later sections you'll need extra time in each day for doing the paying work that comes in as a result of your activities. That time's built in too.

If you're thinking it sounds like a lot of effort, you're right. On most days you'll be working a solid 6-8 hours. You might be tempted to automate some of the tasks, buying in lists or paying someone to execute. **Don't**. Because working on the data *yourself*—drilling methods and models into your head and hands with deliberate practice—will build up a much deeper understanding of how to gain your £100,000 income. Methods you can use for the rest of your life.

Results you win for yourself are better than those any outsider can deliver. Simply because whatever your professional skills are, **you understand them best**. It's that deep understanding of yourself that'll make the 100 Days plan work for you. And keep *on* working. Forever.

///

PARTS 1-4: SETTING UP YOUR BUSINESS

Part 1: Choose your tools lasts one week, and introduces the 7 basic tools and concepts at the core of your 100-day plan. These cover the basics of **web** and **email** marketing with a **List**, **Letter**, and **Campaign**; how to connect with people and turn them into customers with a **search space** and **sales funnel**; and the way 100 Days uses **word processors** and **spreadsheets**. Managed with the methods in Parts **5-7**, your **List** and **Letter** will become core business assets worth a combined £700,000.

Part 2: Define your offer is another one-week stint. It's where you get to **know yourself**: understand what your value proposition *really* is, how it ties together your passion, profession, mission, and vocation, and make the business case to your customers with an **offer to the market**. It's also where you put in the numbers, calculating how many companies you need to contact and people to connect with to drive that £8,350+ in monthly revenues.

Part 3: Find your market also takes a week. In it you'll learn how to *search* and *size* your market in detail: the companies and people most in need of your services. It involves building a **search space** and working out their hopes and dreams, with the goal of putting 1,000 people on your **List** by **Day 100**.

Part 4: Build your network is when you put Parts **1-3** to work, connecting your core offer to your **audience**. Creating a footprint on the web that reaches out to the people you want. . . connecting you to 10m people from a base of 350.

///

PARTS 5-7: CONNECTING TO CUSTOMERS

Part 5: The List also takes a week . . . in one sense. In another sense, it'll take you the rest of your working life! It's about building a **List** with a twist: not just the details of 1,000 or so people able to pay you, but also creating the **metadata** that describes them—so you can communicate with them most effectively.

That's where the value of your **List** comes from—it's a set of companies and contacts that keep your order book stuffed. By **Day 100** it'll be a business asset worth £350,000. (You'll see where that £350,000 figure comes from, too.)

In **Part 6: The Letter** you'll create your second £350,000 business asset, for an eventual total asset value within your business of £700,000. Over two weeks of thinking and deciding, you'll create a **Letter** that appeals to each prospect individually, sentence by sentence and paragraph by paragraph.

This piece of **marketing communication** is what brings in customers forever—with a success rate 10-20x higher than even professional marketing agencies manage for their clients.

Part 7: The Campaign again takes two weeks. In it you'll launch a **marketing campaign** to the first two-thirds or so of your **List**, connecting you to your first customers. You'll learn what actions to take and what numbers to watch to optimise your results over time.

It's about pushing **prospects** down the **sales funnel** you learned in **Part 1** to drive **responses**—from as many as 10% of the 700+ companies and contacts you'll have added to your **List** by then.

///

PARTS 8-10: GETTING THE WORK DONE

Part 8: Prospect to project gets down to business: two weeks in which you'll execute your first **project**, win further projects, and look critically at them all to see how you can win more of the projects that make most sense for you. Time's built into each day for executing the projects you win—but there are still Tasks to be done.

In this Part you'll initiate 5-10 real projects for real people, the start of realising a **Customer Lifetime Value** per client of £100,000 over three years.

Part 9: Project to customer takes winning business two weeks further, with methods for cross-selling and up-selling that lead to customers (and the colleagues they refer) giving you *further* projects.

These customers are ripe for turning into **repeat clients**. You only need 3 repeat clients paying you £2,750 a month, or 8 paying a fraction over £1,000, to blast past your £100,000 target...

...taking you to **Part 10: Customer to retainer**. Days **92** to **98** deal with what you've been working towards for three months: engaging project customers with **retainer agreements** that cover a defined set of monthly tasks for a set fee that keeps rolling for one year.

Your six-figure freelancing career starts here.

ENDGAME AND AFTERMATH

Days **99** and **100** are for looking back and ahead. On **Day 99** you'll **review** your results with a critical eye, and on **Day 100** you'll plan your future: the small and simple tasks, decided by data from your spreadsheet, that you'll turn into daily habits to keep your **List** and **Letter** performing to the max.

Additionally, starting in **Part 4** you'll see **repeated tasks** for each day: the small but significant To-Dos that (over time) build that **£700,000** of business value in your **List** and **Letter**.

Finally, in **Plan your CPD** and some Appendices come a hint of the (other) things that make life and work worthwhile. Freelancing can mean spending a lot of time on your own, and it's important to maintain a sense of connectedness to the world, beyond just keeping your skills sharp.

So next, let's deal with **the biggest barrier to earning £100,000**...

…"WHAT I DO ISN'T WORTH THAT!"

That's the main objection to this book. And it's a self-fulfilling prophecy: **if you believe it, you're right**. So make sure you *don't* think that way.

A research session for 100 Days takes this live, asking a random audience *what they can do*. One by one, the question goes around the lecture room, asking what professional skills people have. There are sales guys, middle managers, financial whizzes. People from engineering firms, software developers, and people in family businesses. Blue collar, white collar, or no collar.

They're all different people, with different areas of expertise. But they have one feature in common: they think their appeal is limited to the same narrow context as a salaried worker. **That's wrong**.

The 100 Days approach demonstrates to the audience how much more their skills *could* be worth, if they start thinking about them in the right way. Some take more thinking about than others, but in the end *every* skill passes the six-figure test. (In other words, everyone in the room could make £100,000 a year from his or her knowledge and experience.) **You are no different**.

SIDEBAR: Finding your proposition

When you approach customers with a personality or positioning that associates you with solving some pain or other, you've got a **value proposition**:

a *process* with an outcome that benefits your customer. The best value proposition is one you're **unconsciously competent** in: you can do the work to a high standard without expending too much effort, thanks to your existing expertise and your love of practicing it.

Your value proposition is how you market yourself, find new prospects, and turn them into lasting customer relationships. Personalities, propositions and positionings are the subject of **Part 2**.

///

At *every* notch on the wage scale, there are hundreds of thousands of experienced professionals—bookkeepers, copywriters, graphic artists, IT contractors, landscape gardeners, lift engineers, motor mechanics, insurance salesmen, office managers. Every one of those pros can earn £100,000+, if they spend 100 days finding the right offer and approaching the right customers. *Every one*.

Chefs aren't in the food business, they're in the experience business. Personal trainers aren't about fitness, they're about confidence. Cleaners aren't about scrubbing floors, they're about healthy homes.

You get to a six-figure income by imagining the business value that results from your work, and how you can best communicate it to the customers who can pay you. That's really all this book's about. Defining your value proposition, then taking it to the people who'll buy again and again.

This book won't make you millions. But like Pirsig's Brick, it *gets you started*.

Let's start now, with **Day 0**.

Day 0: Plan out the plan

> **SUMMARY**
>
> How each day's **outputs** become the next day's **inputs**. Put your 100 Days work plan into your calendar. Start your 100 Days **spreadsheet**. Name your first **worksheet**.

OK, there's a catch. It's 101 days in total. But taking this one day—**Day 0**—before the *real* work starts will get you in the right frame of mind.

There are only two tasks on **Day 0**, but both are vital. First, you'll put your whole 100 days plan in your calendar. And second, you'll have your upper-left-hand brick: your first potential customer.

You'll do both by hand. The first action is to take each Part's summary (the table that says **Part 1: CHOOSE YOUR TOOLS** and similar near the start of each Part in this book) and *put it in your calendar*.

You might think it'd be easier if a handy spreadsheet came free with the book, or if there was a downloadable calendar on 100days100grand.com. But "doing it yourself" is a recurring theme in 100 Days.

As with sets of reps in the gym, it's *repeated actions* that drill the right habits into your head and hands. So never underestimate the power of making your own lists and taking your own actions. Doing the tasks in this book *yourself* is how you build up the daily practices of earning a high income.

Once the tasks are in your calendar, you're more likely to stay on track, with a better sense of whether you're falling behind or keeping ahead of the game. You'll also get a sense of how big this project is, and get your head around what you'll be doing each day.

On to your first Day.

0.1 ADOPT SOME COLOUR CODING

The 10 Parts of **100 Days, 100 Grand** are colour coded titles and tables. If you want to colour your own calendar, here are the web codes for the set of 12. Now let's add a work plan to whatever calendar you use, in your first **Tasks**.

SECTION	COLOUR	HTML
Intro chapters	Red	Hex #800000, RGB 128,0,0 or HSL 0° 100% 25%
Part 1: CHOOSE YOUR TOOLS	Red-orange	Hex #FF4000, RGB 255,64,0 or HSL 15° 100% 50%
Part 2: DEFINE YOUR OFFER	Orange	Hex #FF8000, RGB 255,128,0 or HSL 30° 100% 50%
Part 3: FIND YOUR MARKET	Yellow-orange	Hex #FFBF00, RGB 255,191,0 or HSL 45° 100% 50%
Part 4: BUILD YOUR NETWORK	Yellow	Hex #FFFF00, RGB 255,255,0 or HSL 60° 100% 50%
Part 5: THE LIST	Yellow-green	Hex #808000, RGB 128,128,0 or HSL 60° 100% 25%
Part 6: THE LETTER	Green	Hex #008000, RGB 0,128,0 or HSL 120° 100% 25%
Part 7: THE CAMPAIGN	Blue-green	Hex #008080, RGB 0,128,128 or HSL 180° 100% 25%
Part 8: PROSPECT TO PROJECT	Blue	Hex #000080, RGB 0,0,128 or HSL 240° 100% 25%
Part 9: PROJECT TO CUSTOMER	Blue-violet	Hex #400080, RGB 64,0,128 or HSL 270° 100% 25%
Part 10: CUSTOMER TO RETAINER	Violet	Hex #800080, RGB 128,0,128 or HSL 300° 100% 25%
All other sections	Red-violet	Hex #800040, RGB 128,0,64 or HSL 330° 100% 25%

///

0.2 LEARN TO NAME WORKSHEETS

In today's Tasks you'll set up *100days_yourname_list*, the spreadsheet you'll use to collect and store information about your prospects as they move down the **sales funnel** you'll meet on **Day 6**.

0.2.1 A spreadsheet contains worksheets

You may know a spreadsheet as a two-dimensional grid—and you're right. But a spreadsheet can contain more than one such grid, called **worksheets.**

One grid is one worksheet. You'll create several worksheets in your 100 days, but they'll all be part of a single **spreadsheet**, *100days_yourname_list*.

0.2.2 Each worksheet needs a name

By default, spreadsheets like Excel name worksheets as Sheet1, Sheet2 . . . Sheet*x*. That's not very informative, so an early practice to learn is **renaming**.

To rename a worksheet, simply right-click its name tab at the bottom and hit *Rename*. As you add more worksheets to your spreadsheet, renaming makes it easier to navigate to the worksheet you want, without turning somersaults in your mind working out what *Sheetx* is.

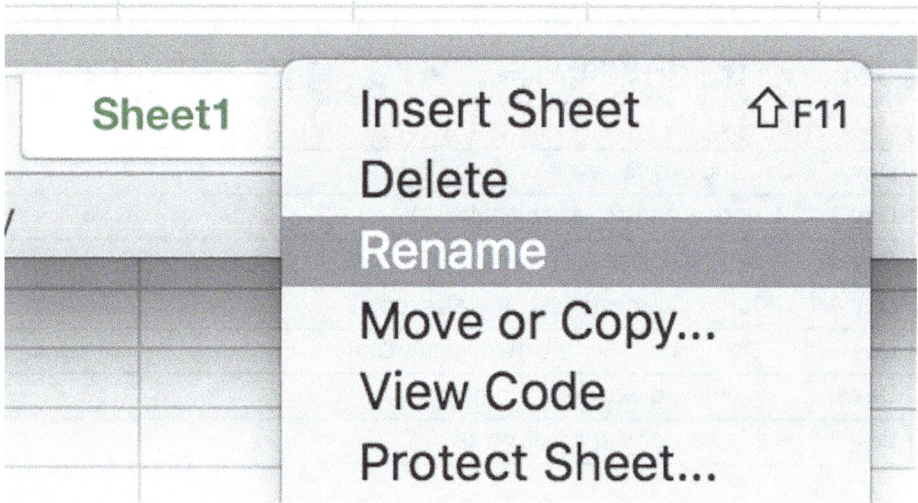

Figure 4: Renaming a worksheet

///

That's today's informational content done. Now let's add a work plan to whatever calendar you use and name the first worksheet in your spreadsheet, in your first **Tasks**.

TASKS: DAY 0

TASK 0.1: PUT THE PLAN IN YOUR CALENDAR

If you use Outlook, Apple Calendar, or Google Docs, here's what to do. It may feel like busywork, but it'll give you a sense of the size of the job in store for the next 100 days, letting you approach each day forewarned and forearmed.

TASK 0.1.1: Label Week 1 as Part 1

1. Decide a day to start your 100-day plan. (Monday works.)
2. Set a new calendar appointment lasting from 10AM Monday to 5PM Sunday.
3. Title it **PART 1: CHOOSE YOUR TOOLS**. If you use colour coding, colour it red-orange as per the colour table.
4. Now return to the first day in that week (Monday). Set another calendar appointment lasting from 10AM to 5PM.
5. Title it with the description of **Day 1**, *Using business networks*.
6. Do the same with the rest of the week: **Day 2**'s title in Tuesday's appointment and so on. Here's the full Part 1 contents table to help:

PART 1: CHOOSE YOUR TOOLS	
Day 1	Using business networks
Day 2	Understanding search engines
Day 3	Setting up your sales website
Day 4	Turning spreadsheets into sales tools
Day 5	Driving documents with dynamic content
Day 6	Managing with a sales funnel
Day 7	Marketing with a mailing list

7. If your application allows subheads, copy in the summary of each Day as the appointment text if you want. Here's **Day 1**'s summary to help.

SUMMARY
About **LinkedIn**. How it connects you to 10m people. The 5 levels of the economy. Its newsfeed and navigation. Your **Profile**. Making **Connections**. Write your LinkedIn **sales headline**.

8. Do the same for each Day of **Part 1**.

9. You've now set your work plan for your first week!

TASK 0.1.2: Label weeks 2-14 as Parts 2-10

1. Go to the next week in your calendar.
2. Do the same as for **Part 1**: a week-long colour-coded appointment titled **PART 2: DEFINE YOUR OFFER** and a day-long appointment with the title of each chapter, for all 7 days of **Part 2**.
3. Repeat for each week until you've got each week's Part and Days in your calendar, with Days **99** and **100** spilling into the fourteenth week at the end. (Remember some Parts take up two weeks.)
4. Here's the colour wheel the book uses, to help you orient yourself.

Figure 5: The 100 Days colour wheel

5. That's your 100-day work plan done! You'll see from your calendar (doesn't it look great?) that it's a series of connected actions over time, each Day a manageable chunk you can start in the morning and finish the same day.

TASK 0.2: START YOUR CUSTOMER LIST

There's a second task on **Day 0**: put a single company on your **List**, to kickstart the £350,000 business asset you'll make use of in **Part 5** and beyond.

TASK 0.2.1: Set up your 100 Days spreadsheet

Check you're familiar with **spreadsheets**. Most label the **columns** (vertical) left-right from A to Z, and the **rows** (horizontal) from 1 to 10,000+ down the left side. This book assumes yours is the same.

TASK 0.2.1.1: Start your 100 Days spreadsheet

1. Wherever you keep files on your computer (such as the Documents folder) start a new folder called **100days**. You'll keep all your **100 Days, 100 Grand** files here.
2. Open a new spreadsheet. Save it as *100days_yourname_list* in directory 100days.
3. You've now created the first of the two principal documents you'll work with over the next 100 days and beyond.

TASK 0.2.1.2: Set up your COMPANIES worksheet

1. Go to your spreadsheet, *100days_yourname_list*. You're going to start and label a worksheet that lists the companies in your market.
2. Rename the default worksheet COMPANIES by right-clicking its name tab (Sheet1) and changing its name. (Uppercase or lowercase as you prefer.)
3. In cell A1 (top left) write COMPANIES as your heading. This is the name of the worksheet. You'll create many more worksheets in this spreadsheet as time goes on, and Row 1 on each worksheet will always contain its name.
4. In cell A2 (below A1), write COMPANY CODE. This is the unique number that'll identify each company on your **List** and connect it to other information you'll add, like people who work there: such identifiers are called **keycodes**.
5. In cell B2 (diagonal down from A1), write COMPANY.
6. In cell C2 (below A2), write ADDR1.
7. In cell D2, write ADDR2.
8. In cell E2, write ADDR3.
9. In cell F2, write ADDR4.
10. In cell G2, write CITY.
11. In cell H2, write COUNTY.
12. In cell I2, write POSTCODE.
13. In cell J2, write COUNTRY.
14. In cell K2, write PHONE.
15. In cell L2, write WEBSITE.

You'll end up with a table like this, with Row 1 containing the worksheet's title and Row 2 containing headings for columns A-L.

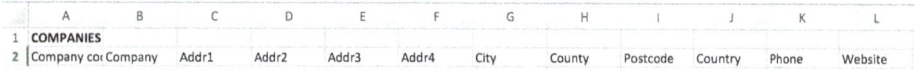

Figure 6: Your PEOPLE headings

TASK 0.2.2: Add the details of one company

Now, of all the companies you know, work for, or just like the look of, think of **one** you'd like to have as a customer of your future freelance business. Just one.

1. In Row 3, cells B3-L3 (leave A3 blank for now) complete *every detail* of that company's main or head office (the address you'd send your invoice to if you worked for it) including switchboard and site.

2. Hit the web if you need to, but under WEBSITE put just the home page address, without http://.

3. In cells B3-F3, when you're filling in the company's address, keep the format consistent. Use ADDR1 and ADDR2 for details like Suite or Building, then ADD3 for the number and street, then ADDR4 for other details like a business park or neighbourhood. (It's OK to leave some columns blank.) Keeping every building number and street in the same column makes the **mailmerging** you'll do from **Part 6** onwards a lot easier.

4. In this company (somewhere) is your first prospective customer. Meaning you've kicked off the spreadsheet that over the next 100 days will grow to 1,000 names.

///

MILESTONE REACHED!
Planned out your 100 days.

MILESTONE REACHED!
Set up your **List** spreadsheet.

Day 0: done. Now read the checklist and make sure you're ready to start **Day 1**.

CHECKLIST: DAY 0	
DO YOU UNDERSTAND:	
Why the Plan works best over 100 days	
The difference between a **spreadsheet** and its **worksheets**	
That a **goal** results from **actions** completed in **sequence**	
That doing it yourself **drills the skills** into your head and hands	
HAVE YOU COMPLETED:	
2 hrs	Added each chapter summary to your calendar
15 mins	Set up and saved your 100 Days spreadsheet
30 mins	Added your first prospect company to your spreadsheet
TAKEOUTS:	
Calendar plan for your next 100 days.	
TOTALS:	
Companies found	**1**
People listed	**0**

ABOUT THE AUTHOR

Chris Worth is a **marketing hobo** who spent a decade with advertising agencies in the capitals of Asia and Europe. Now a six-figure freelancer (obvs) he creates campaigns, copy, and content for clients worldwide—mostly in technology and finance, thanks to a lifelong obsession with STEM subjects (science / technology / engineering / mathematics) and civilisation's drivers philosophy, politics, and economics.

Dropping out at 16, he somehow managed an MBA later in life at the UK's Warwick Business School. Outside interests include literature, architecture, adventure travel, extreme sports, theoretical physics, and all things tech. He also pens the odd thriller as Mark Charteris and sci-fi short as Ted Bann, both more hobbies than jobbies. He's clueless about music, doesn't follow sports, and is a sucker for a box set.

Despite having zero sense of direction, he's explored over 60 countries, from solo treks in Javan jungles to 4x4 jaunts across the Sahara. A keen **boulderer** (climbing without the altitude) and experienced **diver**—scuba *and* sky—he's also a qualified calisthenics and   kettlebells coach who works out daily with bag, bar, 'bells, and body. (The best gym is in your skin.) He practices the close-combat art **Krav Maga** too. (Where the bruises come from.)

His creed is **Objectivism**, the "rules for living" defined by moral philosopher Ayn Rand. Politically he leans **libertarian**: for a limited state that protects individual rights and freedoms. He's also a **minimalist**: after ten years living out of a backpack, the contents of his first house never got beyond bed and bench, while his business infrastructure totals a laptop and phone. The dress code's equally spartan: jeans and a black T. But he's never without his Kindle.

Chris lives in London with his wife Lynne, a polyglot law graduate, finance pro, and foodie with her own series of cookbooks out. Amid the literary haunts of Greenwich and Blackheath, they watch too many movies, enjoy too much food, drink too much wine, and do not enough Yoga to atone for it.

See him at chrisdoescontent.com, amazon.com/author/chrisworth, or head for 100days100grand.com for book updates and reader offers.

INDEX

100 Days spreadsheet, 40

Al Kavadlo, 8

Ayn Rand, 8, 43

Brian Greene, 8

Cal Newport, 8

Chris Worth, 43

COMPANIES worksheet, 40

company, 15, 17, 39, 40, 41, 42

conversion rate, 23

economy, 15, 16, 17, 18, 19, 28, 38

Ernest Hemingway, 8

flow, 8

Kettlebell, 8

Kindle, 11, 43

knowledge, 14, 30, 33

Krav Maga, 43

Letter, 31

List, 31

market, 7, 16, 17, 19, 23, 31, 34, 40

Michael Porter, 8

Mihaly Csikszentmihalyi, 8

MILESTONE REACHED!, 27, 41

mission, 30

passion, 30

Paul "Coach" Wade, 8

person, 15

philosophy, 19, 43

profession, 30

pullup bar, 11

Robert Pirsig, 12

sector, 17

vocation, 30

Watchmen, 8

Figure 7: London's docklands, where freelancers work and play

LIST OF FIGURES

Figure 1: Don't feel trapped by life. Let's go six-figure freelancing.................6

Figure 2: The author and a few friends, somewhere above California 13

Figure 3: Bocconi's "Unique Forms". A solid market offer. 20

Figure 4: Renaming a worksheet..37

Figure 5: The 100 Days colour wheel 39

Figure 6: Your PEOPLE headings..41

Figure 8: London's docklands, where freelancers work and play.................45

See amazon.com/author/chrisworth for works by this author, chrisdoescontent.com for the author's credentials and experience, or 100days100grand.com for book updates and reader offers.

www.ingramcontent.com/pod-product-compliance
Lightning Source LLC
Chambersburg PA
CBHW050715090526
44587CB00019B/3396